SCHOLASTIC

Grades 3–6

EXTRA PRACTICE FOR
Struggling Readers

WORD STUDY

W9-AAV-347

Linda Ward Beech

New York • Toronto • London • Auckland • Sydney
Mexico City • New Delhi • Hong Kong • Buenos Aires

Teaching *Resources*

Editor: Mela Ottaiano
Cover design: Brian LaRossa
Interior design: Melinda Belter
Interior illustrations: Teresa Anderko

ISBN-13: 978-0-545-12411-9
ISBN-10: 0-545-12411-5

Contents

Introduction

Learning to read is *the* goal for all students, but, unfortunately, success is not a given. Many students, for many reasons, find reading an enormous challenge. Despite excellent reading programs, dedicated teachers, and various kinds of interventions, all too many students emerge from the primary grades as struggling readers. One way in which to help these students is with additional practice in word study.

Understanding the structure of words provides useful information to readers when they are figuring out meaning and pronunciation. Elements such as prefixes, suffixes, and roots are invaluable when encountering new words. According to one study, approximately 60 percent of English words have definitions that can be predicted based on the meanings of their parts. Breaking words down into syllables, smaller words, or other word parts helps students recognize common spelling patterns. These skills also support word recognition and vocabulary development. Struggling readers gain confidence as they apply these skills.

By offering opportunities to learn or review basic word study techniques, the lessons in this book help students develop and reinforce reading fluency. You can use the lessons in the sequence given or choose those needed to address specific weaknesses in a student's skills.

Lesson Organization

Each lesson is three pages long and addresses a particular element of word study.

The first lesson page includes:

- a statement of the word study element for the lesson

- examples of the word study element

- a simple activity reinforcing the element

- another exercise

The second page includes:

- two other exercises including cloze exercises, word meaning, identification of word parts, word building, syllables, word endings

The third page includes:

- a word meaning exercise

- a comprehension passage that reviews the lesson element and includes questions; or a word puzzle

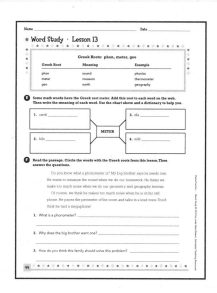

Ways to Make the Most of the Lessons

- Use the lessons in the classroom for extra practice during regular reading time or as individual assignments. Send the lessons home for students to do as homework or to complete with an adult.

- Review, review, review. For example, when students are working on a lesson about prefixes, they will also encounter various vowel and consonant sounds. Take a minute to remind students about what they already know about those sounds.

- Discuss students' answers to clear up misconceptions and to reinforce the lesson element.

- Use the lessons to draw attention to spelling changes for verb tenses or plurals and for parts of speech.

- Have students create word webs to illustrate the use of suffixes, Latin or Greek roots, common syllables, or other word study elements.

- Use the lessons to expand students' vocabulary. Help students use the skills covered in the book to break down the multisyllabic words in the lessons.

- Create word lists from each lesson. Students can use them in word sorts, on word walls, in writing assignments, or in readers' journals.

- Encourage students to write complete sentences when they answer the questions for the comprehension paragraphs in Exercise F.

- Keep observation charts to monitor progress.

★ Word Study · Lesson 1

Compound Words

Some words are made up of two words put together. They are called *compound words*. When you read, look for the words that make up a compound word.

A Write the two words that make up each of the compound words in the box. Then write the compound word.

anthill	teapot	barnyard	birdcage	clothespin
doormat	popcorn	snowflake	toolbox	wheelchair

1. _____ + _____ = _____

2. _____ + _____ = _____

3. _____ + _____ = _____

4. _____ + _____ = _____

5. _____ + _____ = _____

6. _____ + _____ = _____

7. _____ + _____ = _____

8. _____ + _____ = _____

9. _____ + _____ = _____

10. _____ + _____ = _____

B Add the word on the left to each of the words in the row to make compound words.

1. bed _____room _____time _____spread

2. snow _____suit _____storm _____plow

3. foot _____print _____path _____stool

4. eye _____lid _____sight _____ball

Extra Practice . . . Word Study © 2010 by Linda Ward Beech, Scholastic Teaching Resources

★ Word Study · Lesson 1

◆ ★ ◆ ★ ◆ ★ ◆ ★ ◆ ★ ◆ ★ ◆ ★ ◆ ★ ◆ ★ ◆ ★ ◆ ★ ◆ ★ ◆ ★ ◆

C Add the correct word from the box to each group of words to make compound words.

boat	book	day	house

1. cook   + _____   = _____

note   + _____   = _____

pocket + _____   = _____

2. green + _____   = _____

bird   + _____   = _____

light + _____   = _____

3. some   + _____   = _____

every + _____   = _____

birth + _____   = _____

4. tug   + _____   = _____

sail   + _____   = _____

motor + _____   = _____

D Write a compound word to complete each sentence.

1. A case for books is a _____ .

2. A pot for a flower is a _____ .

3. A box for mail is a _____ .

4. A house for a dog is a _____ .

5. A boat that you row is a _____ .

6. A paper with news is a _____ .

Extra Practice . . . Word Study © 2010 by Linda Ward Beech, Scholastic Teaching Resources

★ Word Study · Lesson 1

E **Write a compound word for each riddle.**

Example: Did you ever see a star fish?   starfish

1. Did you ever see a horse fly?   _____

2. Did you ever see a match box?   _____

3. Did you ever see a cat fish?   _____

4. Did you ever see the sun rise?   _____

5. Did you ever see the sea weed?   _____

6. Did you ever see a day dream?   _____

7. Did you ever see hair cut?   _____

8. Did you ever see a door step?   _____

9. Did you ever see a bed roll?   _____

10. Did you ever see milk shake?   _____

F **Read the paragraph and circle the compound words. Then answer the questions.**

Margo likes sports. She keeps her balls in a box in the hallway. Her beachball takes up a lot of space, but her baseball does not. Her football and basketball are also in the box. Where is her skateboard? It's on the floor next to her snowboard.

1. Why does Margo have so many balls? _____

_____

2. Where does she keep them? _____

_____

3. What other sports does Margo like? _____

_____

Extra Practice . . . Word Study © 2010 by Linda Ward Beech, Scholastic Teaching Resources

★ Word Study · Lesson 2

More Compound Words

Some words are made up of two words put together. They are called *compound words*. When you read, look for the words that make up a compound word.

A Write the two words that make up each compound word.

1. footnote   _____ + _____

2. pipeline   _____ + _____

3. barbell   _____ + _____

4. grasshopper   _____ + _____

5. playpen   _____ + _____

6. lawmaker   _____ + _____

7. homeowner   _____ + _____

8. groundwork   _____ + _____

B Write a compound word to complete each sentence.

1. A sleeve for a shirt is a _____ .

2. A skin from a bear is a _____ .

3. Paper for a wall is _____ .

4. A robe for the bath is a _____ .

5. A groom for a bride is a _____ .

6. A chair with an arm is an _____ .

7. The side of a hill is a _____ .

8. A base for data is a _____ .

★ Word Study · Lesson 2

C **Write a compound word for each riddle.**

1. Did you ever see a book shop? _____

2. Did you ever see a bean stalk? _____

3. Did you ever see honey comb? _____

4. Did you ever see a heart break? _____

5. Did you ever see art work? _____

6. Did you ever see a bill fold? _____

D **Read each question. Then circle the best answer.**

1. Which one can fly?   a. **bluefish**   b. **blueberry**   c. **bluebird**

2. Which one can you wear?   a. **raincoat**   b. **raindrop**   c. **rainstorm**

3. Which one is an insect?   a. **housework**   b. **household**   c. **housefly**

4. Which one describes hair?   a. **redcap**   b. **redbird**   c. **redhead**

5. Which one is a machine?   a. **dishwater**   b. **dishtowel**   c. **dishwasher**

6. Which one do you eat?   a. **egghead**   b. **eggplant**   c. **eggshell**

7. Which one is a plant?   a. **catcall**   b. **catnip**   c. **catfish**

8. Which one is part of you?   a. **windmill**   b. **windpipe**   c. **windsock**

9. Which one is news?   a. **headdress**   b. **headboard**   c. **headline**

10. Which one is a person?   a. **landmark**   b. **landlord**   c. **landscape**

Extra Practice . . . . Word Study © 2010 by Linda Ward Beech, Scholastic Teaching Resources

★ Word Study · Lesson 2

E **Think of a word for each picture, then write a compound word.**

1.   + mark = _____

2.   + top = _____

3. sand +   = _____

4. bare +   = _____

5. gold +   = _____

6.   + burn = _____

7. snow + ⬤ = _____

8. copy + 🐈 = _____

9. 🔥 + place = _____

10. 🍎 + sauce = _____

F **Read the paragraph and circle the compound words. Then answer the questions.**

Kirk got out a teaspoon, tablespoon, pan, potholder, and everything else he needed. He opened the cookbook to find the cake he wanted to make. Then he went to work. There was only one setback when he spilled some batter. When the cake was done, Kirk called his mother to the kitchen. "Happy Birthday!" he said. "Here's a homemade cake for you."

1. Why did Kirk want to bake a cake? _____

2. How well did the baking go? _____

3. Was the cake a surprise? Explain your answer. _____

_____

★ Word Study · Lesson 3

Prefixes: un-, re-, over-, mis-, sub-

A prefix is a word part that is added to the beginning of a word. A prefix changes the meaning of a word. Look for prefixes to help you understand what words mean.

Prefix	Meaning	Example
un-	not; opposite of	unfair
re-	again	redo
over-	too much	overcook
mis-	in a wrong way; wrongly	mistreat
sub-	under	subway

A **Study the chart above. Then use it to complete each sentence.**

1. If you cook food too much, you _____ it.

2. If you do something over, you _____ it.

3. If something is not fair, it is _____ .

4. A _____ travels under the ground.

5. If you treat someone wrongly, you _____ that person.

B **Underline the prefix in each word. Then write the base word without the prefix.**

1. unfold _____
2. misuse _____
3. unsafe _____
4. repack _____
5. submarine _____
6. overripe _____

7. misstep _____
8. unsure _____
9. subplot _____
10. overeat _____
11. retie _____
12. rewrite _____

Extra Practice . . . Word Study © 2010 by Linda Ward Beech, Scholastic Teaching Resources

★ Word Study · Lesson 3

Prefixes: un-, re-, over-, mis-, sub-

Prefix	Meaning	Example
un-	not; opposite of	unfair
re-	again	redo
over-	too much	overcook
mis-	in a wrong way; wrongly	mistreat
sub-	under	subway

C Write a heading that tells how each group of words is alike. Then write a meaning for each word.

1. _____

overdo _____

overtip _____

overbake _____

2. _____

reheat _____

refill _____

retell _____

3. _____

unreal _____

unhappy _____

unkind _____

4. _____

misname _____

mislead _____

misnumber _____

D Read each meaning below. Add a prefix to each word in bold type to make a new word.

Meaning	Prefix	+	Word	=	New Word
1. to **call** again					
2. the opposite of **even**					
3. to **flow** too much					
4. under the **soil**					
5. **read** in a wrong way					

★ Word Study · Lesson 3

Prefixes: un-, re-, over-, mis-, sub-

Prefix	Meaning	Example
un-	not; opposite of	unfair
re-	again	redo
over-	too much	overcook
mis-	in a wrong way; wrongly	mistreat
sub-	under	subway

E **Read each question. Then circle the best answer.**

1. Which word means to place wrongly?   a. **replace**   b. **misplace**   c. **placed**

2. Which word means the opposite of loved?   a. **unloved**   b. **lovely**   c. **lover**

3. Which word means pay too much?   a. **underpay**   b. **repay**   c. **overpay**

4. Which word means to use again?   a. **reuse**   b. **used**   c. **overuse**

5. Which word means a heading under another heading?   a. **header**   b. **headed**   c. **subhead**

F **Read the paragraphs and circle the words with prefixes. Then answer the questions.**

Alice tried to enter the room unseen. She was late because she had overslept. But she had misjudged Mr. Hunt.

"What does the subtitle of this chapter mean?" he asked her as she took her seat.

"I'm unsure of what page we're on," said Alice. "Could you restate it for me?"

1. Where does this story take place? _____

2. How did Mr. Hunt show that he wasn't fooled? _____

_____

3. Why doesn't Alice know the answer? _____

Extra Practice . . . Word Study © 2010 by Linda Ward Beech, Scholastic Teaching Resources

★ Word Study · Lesson 4

Prefixes: in-, fore-, de-, dis-, under-

A prefix is a word part that is added to the beginning of a word. A prefix changes the meaning of a word. Look for prefixes to help you understand what words mean.

Prefix	Meaning	Example
in-	not	informal
fore-	before	forewarn
de-	away; take away	defrost
dis-	not; opposite	disobey
under-	below; too little	underpay

A **Study the chart above. Then use it to complete each sentence.**

1. If an event is not formal, it is _____ .

2. If you do not obey, you _____ .

3. If you pay too little, you _____ .

4. If you take away frost from a window, you _____ it.

5. If you warn someone before something happens, you _____ that person.

B **Underline the prefix in each word. Then write a meaning for the word.**

1. indirect _____

2. decontrol _____

3. dislike _____

4. underage _____

5. foretell _____

6. dishonest _____

7. foreground _____

8. dethrone _____

9. underdress _____

★ Word Study · Lesson 4

Prefixes: in-, fore-, de-, dis-, under-

Prefix	Meaning	Example
in-	not	informal
fore-	before	forewarn
de-	away; take away	defrost
dis-	not; opposite	disobey
under-	below; too little	underpay

C **Read each question. Circle the best answer.**

1. Which word means to take
   away a forest? a. **reforest**   b. **deforest**   c. **forester**

2. Which word means
   below water? a. **underwater**   b. **waterfall**   c. **watering**

3. Which word means
   not complete? a. **completely**   b. **completed**   c. **incomplete**

4. Which word means to
   not agree? a. **agreement**   b. **agreeable**   c. **disagree**

5. Which word means a family member
   who lived long before you? a. **father-in-law**   b. **forefather**   c. **fatherly**

D **Read each meaning below. Add a prefix to each word in bold type to make a new word.**

Meaning	Prefix	+	Word	=	New Word
1. not **correct**					
2. to take away **fog**					
3. **charge** too little					
4. opposite of **please**					
5. **see** what might happen before it does					

★ Word Study · Lesson 4

Prefixes: in-, fore-, de-, dis-, under-

Prefix	Meaning	Example
in-	not	informal
fore-	before	forewarn
de-	away; take away	defrost
dis-	not; opposite	disobey
under-	below; too little	underpay

E **Read each question. Then circle the best answer.**

1. Which one means "resting"?　　a. **active**　　b. **proactive**　　c. **inactive**

2. Which one is a mess?　　a. **order**　　b. **disorder**　　c. **reorder**

3. Which one comes first?　　a. **forename**　　b. **surname**　　c. **rename**

4. Which one is too small?　　a. **undersize**　　b. **oversize**　　c. **supersize**

5. Which balloon has no air?　　a. **inflated**　　b. **deflated**　　c. **related**

F **Read the paragraphs and circle the words with prefixes. Then answer the questions.**

Our trouble began at forenoon. Crunch! Our boat got stuck in some thick weeds. You could hear them scrape the underbody. Suddenly, we were disabled.

"This is insane!" said Dad. "This means we have to discontinue our ride.

We'll disembark and swim to shore."

"Okay," said Mom, "but first and foremost, put on your life jackets!"

1. What happened to the boat? _____

_____

2. How did Dad feel about it? _____

_____

3. Who had safety in mind? _____

★ Word Study · Lesson 5

Prefixes: super-, pre-, semi-, multi-, im-

A prefix is a word part that is added to the beginning of a word. A prefix changes the meaning of a word. Look for prefixes to help you understand what words mean.

Prefix	Meaning	Example
super-	of greater degree, size, or importance	superstar
pre-	before	preview
semi-	half	semicircle
multi-	many	multilayered
im-	not	improper

A **Study the chart above. Then use it to complete each sentence.**

1. If something has many layers, it is _____ .

2. If you view something beforehand, you _____ it.

3. If your behavior is not proper, it is _____ .

4. If someone is greater than the usual star, that person is a _____ .

5. If you draw half a circle, you draw a _____ .

B **Choose a word from the box to complete each sentence.
Use the clues below the writing lines to help you.**

1. The stone in that ring is _____ .
   half

2. That water is _____ so don't drink it.
   not

3. He works for a _____ company.
   many

4. We often shop at the _____ .
   greater size

5. She likes to watch the _____ show.
   before

> impure
>
> supermarket
>
> pregame
>
> semiprecious
>
> multinational

Extra Practice . . . Word Study © 2010 by Linda Ward Beech, Scholastic Teaching Resources

★ Word Study · Lesson 5

Prefixes: super-, pre-, semi-, multi-, im-

Prefix	Meaning	Example
super-	of greater degree, size, or importance	superstar
pre-	before	preview
semi-	half	semicircle
multi-	many	multilayered
im-	not	improper

C Read each meaning below. Add a prefix to each word in bold type to make a new word.

Meaning	Prefix	+	Word	=	New Word
1. not **perfect**					
2. greater than usual **man**					
3. to **judge** before					
4. half a **colon**					
5. many **colored**					

D Read the words in the box, then follow the directions.

semifinal	superfine	prepay	overlook	misplace
superhuman	replay	immature	semiannual	impossible
impatient	supernatural	rejoin	semimonthly	prearrange

1. Write the words with the prefix that means "not."

_____

2. Write the words with the prefix that means "half."

_____

3. Write the words with the prefix that means "of greater degree, size, or importance."

_____

★ Word Study · Lesson 5

Prefixes: super-, pre-, semi-, multi-, im-

Prefix	Meaning	Example
super-	of greater degree, size, or importance	superstar
pre-	before	preview
semi-	half	semicircle
multi-	many	multilayered
im-	not	improper

E **Read each question. Then circle the best answer.**

1. Which one comes first? a. **undercook** b. **precook** c. **overcook**

2. Which one is not moving? a. **immobile** b. **mobile** c. **mobility**

3. Which one is biggest? a. **path** b. **road** c. **superhighway**

4. Which one is partly alert? a. **semiconscious** b. **conscious** c. **unconscious**

5. Which one describes a crayon set? a. **multicolored** b. **colorless** c. **colorblind**

F **Read the clues, then complete the puzzle.**

1. A half circle   S _ _ _ _ _ _ _ _

2. Of many cultures   _ _ _ _ _ U _ _ _ _ _

3. Not patient   _ _ P _ _ _ _ _ _

4. Half sweet   _ E _ _ _ _ _ _

5. Date before   _ R _ _ _ _ _ _

6. Greater than most women   _ _ _ _ _ W _ _ _ _

7. Not polite   _ _ _ O _ _ _ _

8. Heat before eating   _ R _ _ _ _ _

9. Many media   _ _ _ _ _ _ D _ _

10. A school for children before
    they start regular school   _ _ _ S _ _ _ _ _

★ Word Study · Lesson 6

Suffixes: -er/or, -ful, -ly, -ness, -able/ible

A suffix is a word part that is added to the end of a word. A suffix changes the meaning of a word. Look for suffixes to help you understand what words mean.

Suffix	Meaning	Example
-er/or	a person who acts as	writer
-ful	full of	joyful
-ly	in that way	sadly
-ness	state of being	rudeness
-able/ible	can be done	washable

A **Study the chart above. Then use it to complete each sentence.**

1. Someone who writes is a _____ .

2. If you speak in a sad way, you speak _____ .

3. If something can be washed, it is _____ .

4. Someone who is rude shows _____ .

5. If you are full of joy, you are _____ .

B **Underline the suffix in each word. Then write the base word without the suffix.**

1. graceful _____
2. fondly _____
3. teacher _____
4. comfortable _____
5. painful _____
6. fairness _____

7. director _____
8. weakly _____
9. skillful _____
10. darkness _____
11. leader _____
12. sweetly _____

★ Word Study · Lesson 6

Suffixes: -er/or, -ful, -ly, -ness, -able/ible

Suffix	Meaning	Example
-er/or	a person who acts as	writer
-ful	full of	joyful
-ly	in that way	sadly
-ness	state of being	rudeness
-able	can be done	washable

C Write a heading telling how each group of words is alike. Then write a meaning for each word.

1. _____

   graceful _____

   hopeful _____

   cheerful _____

2. _____

   rapidly _____

   neatly _____

   quietly _____

3. _____

   fixable _____

   drinkable _____

   beatable _____

4. _____

   banker _____

   builder _____

   climber _____

D Choose a word from the box to complete each sentence. Use the clues to help you.

1. The _____ spoke about his new idea.
   person who acts as

2. The students left the building _____ for the fire drill.
   in that way

3. She worked hard to get over her _____ with people.
   state of being

4. They were _____ not to spill any water.
   full of

5. Is this plastic plate _____ ?
   can be done

careful
breakable
inventor
quickly
shyness

★ Word Study · Lesson 6

Suffixes: -er/or, -ful, -ly, -ness, -able/ible

Suffix	Meaning	Example
-er/or	a person who acts as	writer
-ful	full of	joyful
-ly	in that way	sadly
-ness	state of being	rudeness
-able/ible	can be done	washable

E **Read each question. Then circle the best answer.**

1. Which one is a person?   a. **government**   b. **governor**   c. **governing**

2. Which one describes a puppy?   a. **playful**   b. **playpen**   c. **player**

3. Which one can you taste?   a. **weakness**   b. **sweetness**   c. **dimness**

4. How do you greet a friend?   a. **badly**   b. **madly**   c. **gladly**

5. Which one is a good buy?   a. **beatable**   b. **affordable**   c. **questionable**

F **A pun is a play on words. You can use words with the suffix *-ly* to have pun fun. Complete each sentence with a word from the box. Use the word in bold type as a clue.**

Example: "I make people cry," said the onion tearfully.

1. "The shoe is too **small**," said the stepsister _____ .

2. "It's **hot** today," said the weatherman _____ .

3. "Let's **race**," said the runner _____ .

4. "Turn **off** the light!" said the usher _____ .

5. "My arm is in a **cast**," said the patient _____ .

6. "I am a **werewolf**," said the creature _____ .

7. "May I have the **sugar**?" asked the baker _____ .

8. "I **missed** school," said the student _____ .

sweetly

warmly

bitingly

darkly

absently

brokenly

tightly

swiftly

★ Word Study · Lesson 7

Suffixes: -ship, -ment, -less, -y, -ist

A suffix is a word part that is added to the end of a word. A suffix changes the meaning of a word. Look for suffixes to help you understand what words mean.

Suffix	Meaning	Example
-ship	state of being; rank of	hardship
-ment	action or process	movement
-less	lack of	cloudless
-y	full of	leaky
-ist	one who is or practices	organist

A Study the chart above. Then use it to complete each sentence.

1. Someone who plays the organ is an _____ .

2. A lack of clouds means the sky is _____ .

3. A house that is full of leaks is _____ .

4. The process of moving is _____ .

5. If times are hard, people suffer _____ .

B Read the words in the box, then follow the directions.

1. Write the words with the suffix that means "lack of."

_____

_____

2. Write the words with the suffix that means "action or process."

_____

_____

3. Write the words with the suffix that means "full of."

_____

_____

> ageless placement
>
> misty agreeable
>
> faceless farmer
>
> kingship
>
> treatment
>
> woody gloomy
>
> agreement
>
> fixable careless
>
> illness

★ Word Study · Lesson 7

Suffixes: -ship, -ment, -less, -y, -ist

Suffix	Meaning	Example
-ship	state of being; rank of	hardship
-ment	action or process	movement
-less	lack of	cloudless
-y	full of	leaky
-ist	one who is or practices	organist

C Read each meaning below. Add a suffix to each word in bold type to make a new word.

Meaning	Word	+	Suffix	=	New Word
1. lack of **color**					
2. full of **rain**					
3. process of **develop**ing					
4. rank of **leader**					
5. one who practices the **violin**					

D Choose a word from the box to complete each sentence. Use the clues to help you.

1. The new kitten is still _____ .
   lack of

2. Ted works as a _____ for a newspaper.
   one who is

3. After the rain, the air turned _____ .
   full of

4. We made an _____ to see the doctor.
   action or process

5. Your _____ means a lot to me.
   state of being

journalist

appointment

nameless

full of

friendship

steamy

★ Word Study · Lesson 7

Suffixes: -ship, -ment, -less, -y, -ist

Suffix	Meaning	Example
-ship	state of being; rank of	hardship
-ment	action or process	movement
-less	lack of	cloudless
-y	full of	leaky
-ist	one who is or practices	organist

E **Read each question. Then circle the best answer.**

1. Which one is competing?   a. **dentist**   b. **finalist**   c. **realist**

2. Which one is bald?   a. **hairless**   b. **hairy**   c. **hairnet**

3. Which one is in
   Washington, D.C.?   a. **governor**   b. **government**   c. **governess**

4. Which one is good
   for sailing?   a. **windmill**   b. **windfall**   c. **windy**

5. Which one means
   "playing fair"?   a. **sporty**   b. **sportsmanship**   c. **sportscaster**

F **Read the paragraph and circle the words with suffixes. Then answer the questions.**

My mother is a naturalist and spends a lot of time in the desert. She finds great contentment is this timeless environment. I think she is lucky to get such enjoyment from her job. But as for me, I hope to get an internship with a forest ranger this summer. I think working in a cool, leafy forest would be a great arrangement.

1. How does the mother feel about her job? _____

2. What kinds of environments does the writer mention? _____

   _____

3. Why do you think the writer prefers working with a forest ranger? _____

   _____

Name _____   Date _____

★ Word Study · Lesson 8

Suffixes: -ant/ent, -al, -ous, -ion/tion, -hood

A suffix is a word part that is added to the end of a word. A suffix changes the meaning of a word. Look for suffixes to help you understand what words mean.

Suffix	Meaning	Example
-ant/ent	a person who	assistant
-al	relating to	seasonal
-ous	having qualities of	marvelous
-ion/tion	act or process	collection
-hood	state of being	knighthood

A Study the chart above. Then use it to complete each sentence.

1. The act of collecting results in a _____ .

2. A person who assists is an _____ .

3. Something that relates to a season is _____ .

4. Someone who is a knight has a _____ .

5. If something is a marvel, it is _____ .

B Underline the suffix in each word. Then write the base word.

1. clinical _____

2. defendant _____

3. protection _____

4. attendant _____

5. adulthood _____

6. national _____

7. joyous _____

8. humorous _____

9. rejection _____

10. sisterhood _____

11. comical _____

12. action _____

★ Word Study · Lesson 8

Suffixes: -ant/ent, -al, -ous, -ion/tion, -hood

Suffix	Meaning	Example
ant/ent-	a person who	assistant
al-	relating to	seasonal
ous-	having qualities of	marvelous
ion/tion-	act or process	collection
hood-	state of being	knighthood

C **Read each meaning below. Add a suffix to each word in bold type to make a new word.**

Meaning	Word	+	Suffix	=	New Word
1. someone who is in a contest					
2. relating to the coast					
3. the state of a child					
4. having the qualities of danger					
5. the process of attracting					

D **Choose a word from the box to complete each sentence. Use the clues to help you.**

1. After she had children, Mrs. Tully wrote a book about _____ .

   state of being

2. This is a copy, not the _____ painting.

   relating to

3. When she reread her paper, Angie made a _____ .

   act or process

4. To be an explorer, you must be _____ .

   having qualities of

5. Roger was proud when he was elected _____ .

   a person who

president

correction

original

motherhood

adventurous

★ Word Study · Lesson 8

Suffixes: -ant/ent, -al, -ous, -ion/tion, -hood

Suffix	Meaning	Example
ant/ent-	a person who	assistant
al-	relating to	seasonal
ous-	having qualities of	marvelous
ion/tion-	act or process	collection
hood-	state of being	knighthood

E **Read each question. Then circle the best answer.**

1. Which one is a newcomer?   a. **immigration**   b. **immigrant**   c. **immigrate**

2. Which one could be an aunt?   a. **relation**   b. **relate**   c. **unrelated**

3. Which one is a place?   a. **neighborhood**   b. **neighborly**   c. **neighbor**

4. Which one is a retreat?   a. **withdrawn**   b. **withhold**   c. **withdrawal**

5. Which one is a big event?   a. **momentarily**   b. **momentous**   c. **moment**

F **Read the paragraph and circle the words with suffixes. Then answer the questions.**

During my boyhood, my father sent me to be a servant to a knight. This knight had a thunderous voice and was a champion at arms. At first, my reaction to him was fear, but I soon found he had a good heart. The years I spent with him were very educational. When my time with him was up, I knew that I, too, hoped for a knighthood.

1. How did the writer spend his boyhood? _____

_____

2. Why was the writer afraid of the knight at first? _____

_____

3. Why do you think the knight was a good example to the boy? _____

_____

★ Word Study · Lesson 9

Prefixes and Suffixes

Some words are long because they have both a prefix and a suffix. Look for prefixes and suffixes to help you understand what a word means.

A **Write the prefix and the suffix in each word. Then write the base word.**

	Prefix	Suffix	Base Word
1. reaction			
2. nonsmoker			
3. unsinkable			
4. overpayment			
5. foreseeable			
6. disagreement			
7. unbeatable			
8. indirectness			
9. nonsupporter			
10. mistreatment			

B **Choose a word from the box to complete each sentence.**

1. Something that you can return to a store is _____ .

2. When you renew a membership, it is a _____ .

3. An _____ is an act that is not kind.

4. When you pay back a loan, you make a _____ .

5. If something is not perfect, it has an _____ .

renewal

imperfection

returnable

unkindness

repayment

★ Word Study · Lesson 9

C **Read the words in the box, then follow the directions.**
You can use a word more than once.

1. Write the words that have a prefix that means "not."

   _____

   _____

2. Write the words that have a suffix that means "state of being."

   _____

   _____

3. Write the words that have a prefix that means "before."

   _____

   _____

nonpayment
unreadable
forerunner
unevenness
preschooler
unfairness
immovable
prepayment

D **Read each question. Then circle the best answer.**

1. Which word means "able to be used again"?

   a. **usable**   b. **reusable**   c. **unusable**

2. Which word means "before the time of written history"?

   a. **prehistory**   b. **historical**   c. **historian**

3. Which word means "no action"?

   a. **action**   b. **active**   c. **inaction**

4. Which word means "twice a week"?

   a. **semiweekly**   b. **weekly**   c. **weekend**

5. Which word means "something that has been stated again"?

   a. **statement**   b. **misstatement**   c. **restatement**

★ Word Study · Lesson 9

E **Read each question. Then circle the best answer.**

1. Which one is a young child?   a. **preschool**   b. **preschooler**   c. **schoolroom**

2. Which one is really bad?   a. **bearable**   b. **bearing**   c. **unbearable**

3. Which one is against the law?   a. **unlawful**   b. **lawyer**   c. **lawful**

4. Which behavior is rude?   a. **politely**   b. **impolitely**   c. **polite**

5. Which one is an accident?   a. **railed**   b. **railroad**   c. **derailment**

F **Read the paragraphs and circle the words with both a prefix and a suffix. Then answer the questions.**

Suki thought the paper cups she bought for the party were unbreakable. She didn't see the imperfection in the one she held.

"You need a replacement," said Jorge with disapproval. "That cup is unusable. It has a rip in it!"

Suki's unhappiness showed on her face. "I'll have to take them all back," she said impatiently.

1. Why does Suki have to take the cups back? _____

_____

2. How does Jorge feel about the cups Suki bought? _____

_____

3. How does Suki feel about taking the cups back? _____

_____

★ Word Study · Lesson 10

Latin Roots: ped, numer, act, port, art

Many words in English come from Latin. If you know the meaning of Latin roots, it will help you understand these words when you read.

Latin Root	Meaning	Example
ped	foot	pedal
numer	number	numeral
act	do	action
port	carry	porter
art	skill	artist

A **Study the chart above. Then use it to complete each sentence.**

1. A _____ is someone who carries suitcases.

2. You use your feet to _____ a bike.

3. An _____ is skilled at art.

4. When people take _____ , they do things.

5. Something that stands for a number is a _____ .

B **Underline the Latin root in each word. Then write a meaning for the word. Use the chart above and a dictionary to help you.**

1. artistic _____

2. pedestrian _____

3. numerous _____

4. active _____

5. portable _____

C **Choose a word from the box to complete each sentence.**

1. A base on which a statue stands is a _____ .

2. Ships _____ goods from place to place.

3. A skilled worker is an _____ .

| transport |
| pedestal |
| artisan |

★ Word Study · Lesson 10

Latin Roots: ped, numer, act, port, art

Latin Root	Meaning	Example
ped	foot	pedal
numer	number	numeral
act	do	action
port	carry	porter
art	skill	artist

D **Read the words below, then follow the directions.**

acting	activist
import	artful
deport	activism
transact	artificial
enumerate	
numerical	
pedicure	
pedometer	
numerology	

1. Write the words with the Latin root that means "carry."

   _____

2. Write the words with the Latin root that means "foot."

   _____

3. Write the words with the Latin root that means "skill."

   _____

4. Write the words with the Latin root that means "do."

   _____

5. Write the words with the Latin root that means "number."

   _____

E **Read each question. Then circle the best answer.**

1. Which one is for walkers?   a. **thermometer**   b. **odometer**   c. **pedometer**

2. Which one is in a fraction?   a. **numerator**   b. **operator**   c. **radiator**

3. Which one gets things going?   a. **deactivate**   b. **activate**   c. **elevate**

4. Which one includes cars and trucks?   a. **transparency**   b. **translation**   c. **transportation**

5. Which one is made with skill?   a. **archer**   b. **artifact**   c. **artichoke**

★ Word Study · Lesson 10

Latin Roots: ped, numer, act, port, art

Latin Root	Meaning	Example
ped	foot	pedal
numer	number	numeral
act	do	action
port	carry	porter
art	skill	artist

F Read the clues. Then use the words below to complete the puzzle.

actor	exports	portfolio	pedaling	moped
numbers	artmobile	numerical	artwork	reaction

1. A container for carrying papers   _ _ _ _ _ _ L _ _

2. She is _____ to make the paddle boat move.   _ _ _ A _ _ _ _

3. What people hang on walls   _ _ T _ _ _ _

4. Relating to numbers   _ _ _ _ _ I _ _ _

5. An action in response to an action   _ _ _ _ _ _ N _

6. Goods carried out of a country for sale   _ _ _ _ _ R _ _

7. A van carrying art   _ _ _ _ O _ _ _

8. A bike with a motor   _ _ O _ _

9. Someone who does things on a stage   _ _ T _ _

10. Symbols used for counting   _ _ _ _ _ _ S

★ Word Study · Lesson 11

Latin Roots: pop, form, ject, nav, man

Many words in English come from Latin. If you know the meaning of Latin roots, it will help you understand these words when you read.

Latin Root	Meaning	Example
pop	people	population
form	shape	formula
ject	throw	reject
nav	ship	navy
man	hand	manual

A Study the chart above. Then use it to complete each sentence.

1. A branch of the armed forces with ships is a _____ .

2. Work that is done by hand is _____ labor.

3. The number of people in a city is its _____ .

4. If you toss rotten apples away, you _____ them.

5. A _____ is a set of words that tells how to make something.

B Read the words in the box, then follow the directions.

1. Write the words with the Latin root that means "throw."

   _____

   _____

2. Write the words with the Latin root that means "hand."

   _____

   _____

3. Write the words with the Latin root that means "shape.

   _____

   _____

inject
transform
deform
manage
rejection
formation
projection
manufacture

★ Word Study · Lesson 11

Latin Roots: pop, form, ject, nav, man

Latin Root	Meaning	Example
pop	people	population
form	shape	formula
ject	throw	reject
nav	ship	navy
man	hand	manual

C **Choose a word from the box to complete each sentence.**

1. A vending machine can _____ cans of juice.

2. A treatment for hands and nails is a _____ .

3. A _____ area is full of people.

4. A cloud is a _____ of raindrops.

5. The captain of a warship is a _____ officer.

> manicure
>
> formation
>
> naval
>
> eject
>
> populous

D **Underline the Latin root in each word. Then circle the best meaning for the word.**

1. **popular**   a. something you write on   b. liked by many people   c. a spicy black seasoning

2. **formless**   a. without shape   b. a farm worker   c. hardness

3. **manacle**   a. of the mind   b. a ruler   c. a handcuff

4. **navigate**   a. to begin   b. to steer a ship   c. to avoid taking sides

5. **objective**   a. quick to notice   b. something in the way   c. something you aim at

★ Word Study · Lesson 11

Latin Roots: pop, form, ject, nav, man

Latin Root	Meaning	Example
pop	people	population
form	shape	formula
ject	throw	reject
nav	ship	navy
man	hand	manual

E **Read each question. Then circle the best answer.**

1. Which one do you wear?   a. **uniform**   b. **reform**   c. **conform**

2. Which one is a person?   a. **manuscript**   b. **manager**   c. **manure**

3. Which one is blue?   a. **navy**   b. **lime**   c. **rose**

4. Which one is about sadness?   a. **perfection**   b. **correction**   c. **dejection**

5. Which music is the newest?   a. **blues**   b. **pop**   c. **folk**

F **Read the paragraphs and circle the words with the Latin roots from this lesson. Then answer the questions.**

Olive decided to get a haircut and a manicure.

"Transform me," she told the beauty shop owner. "I am going to a formal dinner on the naval base. My date is an officer in the Navy."

The hairdresser put on her uniform. "Let's begin," she said. "You'll look great when we are done."

"Don't worry," added the manicurist. "You will be very popular. No one will reject you."

1. What did Olive want at the beauty shop? _____

_____

2. Why did she want to look good? _____

_____

3. How was she treated at the shop? _____

★ Word Study · Lesson 12

Latin Roots: vis/vid, dict, aud, liber, mar

Many words in English come from Latin. If you know the meaning of Latin roots, it will help you understand these words when you read.

Latin Root	Meaning	Example
vis/vid	see	vision
dict	say	predict
aud	hear	audio
liber	free	liberty
mar	sea	marina

A **Study the chart above. Then use it to complete each sentence.**

1. After he did his homework, Russ was at _____ to play baseball.

2. Take care of your eyes because your _____ is important.

3. The boat sailed from the sea to the _____ to dock.

4. You can listen to _____ books in the car.

5. If you _____ something, you say what will happen before it does.

B **Read the words, then follow the directions.**

1. Write the words with the Latin root that means "sea."

   _____

2. Write the words with the Latin root that means "free."

   _____

3. Write the words with the Latin root that means "hear."

   _____

4. Write the words with the Latin root that means "say."

   _____

5. Write the words with the Latin root that means "see."

   _____

audible
liberate
mariner
liberal
vista
auditory
video
maritime
dictate
prediction

★ Word Study · Lesson 12

Latin Roots: vis/vid, dict, aud, liber, mar

Latin Root	Meaning	Example
vis/vid	see	vision
dict	say	predict
aud	hear	audio
liber	free	liberty
mar	sea	marina

C **Underline the Latin root in each word. Then circle the best meaning for the word.**

1. **contradict**   a. to contribute   b. to say the opposite   c. to shorten a pair of words

2. **marine**   a. related to the sea   b. a kind of sheep   c. a way of doing things

3. **audience**   a. fall season   b. group of listeners   c. a sale to bidders

4. **visualize**   a. to pay a visit   b. to be a good person   c. to form a mental picture

5. **liberally**   a. happily   b. freely   c. quietly

D **Choose a word from the box to complete each sentence.**

1. A _____ tells you how to pronounce words.

2. If something is _____ , you can't hear it.

3. A _____ is someone who frees people.

4. If you soak meat in a liquid, you _____ it.

5. Things that you can see are _____ .

> visible
>
> marinate
>
> dictionary
>
> inaudible
>
> liberator

★ Word Study · Lesson 12

Latin Roots: vis/vid, dict, aud, liber, mar

Latin Root	Meaning	Example
vis/vid	see	vision
dict	say	predict
aud	hear	audio
liber	free	liberty
mar	sea	marina

E **Read each question. Then circle the best answer.**

1. Which one is about words?   a. **faction**   b. **suction**   c. **diction**

2. Which one shades your eyes?   a. **visor**   b. **razor**   c. **scissor**

3. Which one is a famous statue?   a. **liberty**   b. **injury**   c. **sanity**

4. Which one is for concerts?   a. **playground**   b. **auditorium**   c. **supermarket**

5. Which one moves underwater?   a. **bicycle**   b. **submarine**   c. **airplane**

F **Read the paragraphs and circle the words with the Latin roots from this lesson. Then answer the questions.**

Sari's cat got stuck in a tree, and his meows were very audible. Bad cat! By the time Sari liberated him, she was late—late for her big chance. Sari was going to an audition for a new television show. Now she could just predict what would happen. Someone else would get the part. No! She couldn't let that happen.

Quickly, Sari jumped into her boat and sped across the marina. On her way she envisioned how she would explain her lateness and maybe get another chance.

1. Why was Sari late? _____

2. Where was she going? _____

3. Do you think she got a chance to audition? Explain. _____

_____

★ Word Study · Lesson 13

Greek Roots: phon, meter, geo

Many words in English come from Greek. If you know the meaning of Greek roots, it will help you understand more words when you read.

Greek Root	Meaning	Example
phon	sound	phonics
meter	measure	thermometer
geo	earth	geography

A **Study the chart above. Then use it to complete each sentence. You may use a word more than once.**

1. A _____ measures temperature.

2. The study of earth's surface is called _____ .

3. In reading, you learn about _____ , the sounds that letters spell.

4. To find out how warm it is, check a _____ .

5. You learn about earth's plains, hills, and mountains in _____ .

B **Choose a word from the box to complete each sentence.**

earphones	geologist	metronome	speedometer	telephone

1. Someone who studies earth's crust is a _____ .

2. A _____ measures the speed of a car.

3. He used _____ to listen to music.

4. A _____ measures or marks time for a musician.

5. You can talk to a friend on the _____ .

Extra Practice . . . Word Study © 2010 by Linda Ward Beech, Scholastic Teaching Resources

★ Word Study · Lesson 13

Greek Roots: phon, meter, geo

Greek Root	Meaning	Example
phon	sound	phonics
meter	measure	thermometer
geo	earth	geography

C Underline the Greek root in each word below. Then write a meaning for each word. Use the chart above and a dictionary to help you.

1. geode _____

2. odometer _____

3. megaphone _____

4. perimeter _____

5. geology _____

D Underline the Greek root in each word. Then circle the best meaning for the word.

1. **microphone**   a. instrument to make sound louder   b. film for making small photos   c. a kind of germ

2. **pedometer**   a. someone who takes care of feet   b. instrument to measure walking distance   c. a triangular part of a building

3. **geocentric**   a. very large   b. related to exercise   c. viewed from earth's center

4. **symphony**   a. place of worship   b. music for an orchestra   c. a sameness of feeling

5. **barometer**   a. something left over   b. instrument to measure air pressure   c. having to do with the eye

★ Word Study · Lesson 13

Greek Roots: phon, meter, geo		
Greek Root	**Meaning**	**Example**
phon	sound	phonics
meter	measure	thermometer
geo	earth	geography

Some math words have the Greek root *meter*. Add this root to each word on the web. Then write the meaning of each word. Use the chart above and a dictionary to help you.

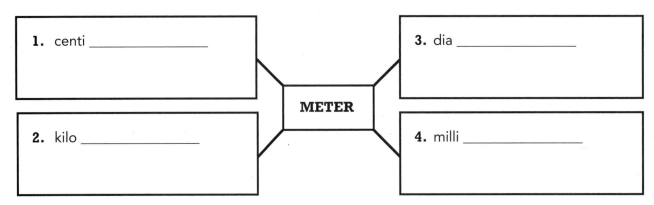

1. centi _____

2. kilo _____

METER

3. dia _____

4. milli _____

Read the passage. Circle the words with the Greek roots from this lesson. Then answer the questions.

Do you know what a phonometer is? My big brother says he needs one. He wants to measure the sound when we do our homework. He thinks we make too much noise when we do our geometry and geography lessons.

Of course, we think he makes too much noise when he is on his cell phone. He paces the perimeter of the room and talks in a loud voice. You'd think he had a megaphone!

1. What is a phonometer? _____

_____

2. Why does the big brother want one? _____

_____

3. How do you think this family should solve this problem? _____

_____

★ Word Study · Lesson 14

Greek Roots: photo, auto, bio

Many words in English come from Greek. If you know the meaning of Greek roots, it will help you understand these words when you read.

Greek Root	Meaning	Example
photo	light	photograph
auto	self	automobile
bio	life	biology

A **Study the chart above. Then use it to complete each sentence. You may use a word more than once.**

1. An _____ moves on its own power.

2. The study of living things is called _____ .

3. In a _____ , film is exposed to light.

4. You might learn about plants and animals in a _____ class.

5. The invention of the _____ changed the way people travel.

B **Choose a word from the box to complete each sentence.**

autocade   photocopier   biohazard   autograph   biography

1. Have you ever asked a rock star to sign an _____ ?

2. A _____ is someone's life story.

3. A procession of cars is an _____ .

4. You can reproduce a photo on a _____ .

5. A _____ can cause health problems.

★ Word Study · Lesson 14

Greek Roots: photo, auto, bio

Greek Root	Meaning	Example
photo	light	photograph
auto	self	automobile
bio	life	biology

C **Underline the Greek root in each word. Then circle the best meaning for the word.**

1. biographer a. writer of a life story b. a follower c. a kind person

2. photogenic a. a very smart person b. photographs well c. a loud sound

3. automotive a. a rock slide b. a way to measure c. self-moving

4. automatic a. relating to fall b. to give power c. self-operating

5. biome a. pair of field glasses b. community of living things c. field of engineering

D **Read the words, then follow the directions.**

telephoto	biopsy	photostat	automation
autobus	biosphere	photocopy	biological
biofeedback	photoplay	photographer	automat

1. Write the words with the Greek root that means "life."

_____

2. Write the words with the Greek root that means "light."

_____

3. Write the words with the Greek root that means "self."

_____

★ Word Study · Lesson 14

Greek Roots: photo, auto, bio

Greek Root	Meaning	Example
photo	light	photograph
auto	self	automobile
bio	life	biology

E **Read each question. Then circle the best answer.**

1. Which one is a life scientist?   a. **artist**   b. **violinist**   c. **biologist**

2. Which one writes about herself?   a. **biographer**   b. **grasshopper**   c. **autobiographer**

3. Which one uses light?   a. **telegraph**   b. **photograph**   c. **autograph**

4. Which one is about life on earth?   a. **biosphere**   b. **hemisphere**   c. **unisphere**

5. Which one is a lightbulb?   a. **flash flood**   b. **folklore**   c. **photoflash**

F **Read the paragraph and circle the words with the Greek roots from this lesson. Then answer the questions.**

The students in Miss Hull's class were learning about careers. Jan wanted to be a photographer. Miles wanted to design automobiles. Cindy said she would be a movie star and sign autographs for fans. Other students were interested in biology and biochemistry careers. Sonny said he would be an author and write a biography for each classmate who became famous.

1. Why were the students talking about the work they wanted to do?

_____

2. What skills do you think Miles would need for his career?

_____

3. What advice would you give to these students about succeeding in their careers?

_____

★ Word Study · Lesson 15

Greek Roots: graph, tele, cycle

Many words in English come from Greek. If you know the meaning of Greek roots, it will help you understand these words when you read.

Greek Root	Meaning	Example
graph	write	autograph
tele	far	telescope
cyclo	wheel	cycle

A **Study the chart above. Then use it to complete each sentence. You may use a word more than once.**

1. The seasons come and go in a never-ending _____ .

2. The soccer player signed his _____ on my program.

3. You can see the stars through a _____ .

4. We can _____ around the park tomorrow.

5. A powerful lens helps you see through this _____ .

B **Underline the Greek root from this lesson in each word. Then write a meaning for the word. Use the chart above and a dictionary to help you.**

1. recycle _____

2. telephoto _____

3. telephone _____

4. graphic _____

5. graphite _____

★ Word Study · Lesson 15

Greek Roots: graph, tele, cycle

Greek Root	Meaning	Example
graph	write	autograph
tele	far	telescope
cyclo	wheel	cycle

C **Choose a word from the box to complete each sentence.**

cyclical	telegram	graphology	cyclist	televise

1. What station will _____ the game tonight?

2. Selling bathing suits is a _____ business.

3. In the old movie, people sent messages by _____ .

4. The study of handwriting is called _____ .

5. In a race, each _____ rides as part of a team.

D **Some words have more than one Greek part. Write each Greek part for the words below.**

1. geography _____   4. telemeter _____

2. telegraph _____   5. telephoto _____

3. autograph _____

E **Read each question. Then circle the best answer.**

1. Which one is a person?   a. **geographic**   b. **geographer**   c. **geography**

2. Which one is a storm?   a. **cyclone**   b. **cycling**   c. **unicycle**

3. Which one is a machine?   a. **telegenic**   b. **teledrama**   c. **television**

4. Which one has wheels?   a. **triceps**   b. **tricycle**   c. **triangle**

★ Word Study · Lesson 15

Greek Roots: graph, tele, cycle

Greek Root	Meaning	Example
graph	write	autograph
tele	far	telescope
cyclo	wheel	cycle

F **Read the clues, then use the words below to complete the puzzle.**

telegraph   bicyclist   graphic   telephone   bicycle

phonograph   biography   autograph   televise   telescope

1. A machine you play records on
    _ _ _ _ _ G _ _ _

2. Someone's life story
    _ _ _ _ _ R _ _ _

3. Bike is short for the word ___ .
    _ _ _ _ _ E _

4. Relating to written material
    _ _ _ A _ _ _

5. What you use to call someone
    T _ _ _ _ _ _ _ _

6. An outdated way of sending short messages
    _ _ _ _ R _ _ _

7. An instrument for looking at stars.
    _ _ _ _ O _ _ _ _

8. Someone's signature
    _ _ _ O _ _ _ _

9. To put something on television
    T _ _ _ _ _ _

10. Someone who rides a bike
    _ _ _ _ _ S _

★ Word Study · Lesson 16

Greek and Latin Number Roots

Many Greek and Latin roots are related to numbers. If you know the meaning of these roots, it will help you understand words containing them when you read.

Greek Root	Latin Root	Meaning	Example
monos	unus/uni	one	monorail unicorn
	bi	two	bicycle
tri		three	triplex
	quartus	four	quartet
	decem	ten	decade
	centum	hundred	century

A **Study the chart above. Then use it to complete each sentence.**

1. *Tri* means "three," so a triplex has _____ floors.

2. *Quartus* means "four," so a quartet has _____ members.

3. *Centum* means "hundred," so a century has one _____ years.

4. *Monos* means "one," so a monorail has one _____ rail.

5. *Uni* means "one," so a unicorn has _____ horn.

6. *Bi* means "two," so a bicycle has _____ wheels.

7. *Decem* means "ten," so a decade has _____ years.

B **Circle the number root in each word below. Then write the meaning of the root.**

1. centipede _____

2. bisect _____

3. monopoly _____

4. triple _____

5. biweekly _____

6. union _____

7. trio _____

★ Word Study · Lesson 16

Greek and Latin Number Roots

Greek Root	Latin Root	Meaning	Example
monos	unus/uni	one	monorail unicorn
	bi	two	bicycle
tri		three	triplex
	quartus	four	quartet
	decem	ten	decade
	centum	hundred	century

C **Choose a word from the box to complete each sentence.**

decagon   unanimous   quadruplet   centenarian   bilingual   trident   monocle

1. A _____ is someone who is 100 years old.

2. A _____ has three prongs.

3. When a vote is _____ , all vote as one.

4. A _____ is an eyeglass for one eye.

5. A _____ is one of four children born at the same time.

6. Someone who can speak two languages is _____ .

7. A _____ has ten sides and ten angles.

D **Use the chart at the top of the page to help you answer each question.**

1. How many points in a quadrangle? _____

2. How many wheels on a unicycle? _____

3. How many subjects in a monograph? _____

4. How many books in a trilogy? _____

5. How many events for an athlete in a decathlon? _____

6. How many centimeters in a meter? _____

★ Word Study · Lesson 16

Greek and Latin Number Roots

Greek Root	Latin Root	Meaning	Example
monos	unus/uni	one	monorail unicorn
	bi	two	bicycle
tri		three	triplex
	quartus	four	quartet
	decem	ten	decade
	centum	hundred	century

E **Read each question. Then circle the best answer.**

1. Which tooth has two cusps?   a. **incisor**   b. **molar**   c. **bicuspid**

2. Which group is a threesome?   a. **twins**   b. **triplets**   c. **dozen**

3. Which poem has four lines?   a. **couplet**   b. **quatrain**   c. **haiku**

4. Which one has the fewest syllables?   a. **compound**   b. **monosyllable**   c. **multisyllable**

5. Which one is a quadruped?   a. **horse**   b. **chicken**   c. **octopus**

F **Read the paragraphs and circle the words with Greek or Latin number roots. Then answer the questions.**

Our town is about to celebrate its centennial. The school band has new uniforms for marching in the parade. I plan to borrow my uncle's binoculars to watch the bands and floats go by.

There will be other entertainment as well. I read about a barbershop quartet, a brass trio, and even a unicycle act. After that there will be a stand-up comedian who does a funny monologue. I can't wait!

1. Why is the town planning so much entertainment? _____

_____

2. How does the writer plan to see things? _____

_____

3. When will the town celebrate its next centennial? _____

★ Word Study · Lesson 17

Plurals

The plural form of a noun is spelled differently than the singular form. When you read, look to see if a noun is singular or plural.

Type of Plural	Examples
Most plural nouns have an *s* at the end.	books
Nouns that end in *sh, ch, x, s,* or *ss* have *es* at the end for their plural form.	dishes, lunches, boxes, circuses, guesses
Nouns that end in a consonant and *y* drop the *y* and have *ies* at the end for their plural form.	pennies

A Study the chart above. Then use it to help you find and circle the plural noun in each sentence.

1. Ming put the dishes on the table.

2. How many peaches did you bring to the picnic?

3. The teacher read two stories aloud.

4. The buses were lined up by the curb.

5. The boys ran into the gym.

6. Kevin put his glasses in a case.

7. The mailboxes are in the lobby.

B Write the plural form for each word below. Use the chart to help you.

1. berry _____

2. mess _____

3. mix _____

4. computer _____

5. match _____

6. octopus _____

7. eyelash _____

8. hobby _____

Extra Practice . . . Word Study © 2010 by Linda Ward Beech, Scholastic Teaching Resources

★ Word Study · Lesson 17

Plurals

Type of Plural	Examples
Most plural nouns have an *s* at the end.	books
Nouns that end in *sh*, *ch*, *x*, *s*, or *ss* have *es* at the end for their plural form.	dishes, lunches, boxes, circuses, guesses
Nouns that end in a consonant and *y* drop the *y* and have *ies* at the end for their plural form.	pennies

C **Fill in the circle next to the word that best tells about each picture.**

1.

   ○ puppy

   ○ poppy

   ○ puppies

2. ○ bush

   ○ brush

   ○ brushes

3. ○ fixes

   ○ foxes

   ○ fox

4.

   ○ walrus

   ○ walnut

   ○ walruses

5.

   ○ church

   ○ churches

   ○ chuckles

6.

   ○ dress

   ○ dishes

   ○ dresses

D **Circle the correct word to complete each sentence.**

1. Noah played several _____ on the piano.   melody   melodies

2. The girls planned to go to the _____ on Saturday.   beach   beaches

3. There were three _____ to the accident.   witness   witnesses

4. People pay state and federal _____ in April.   tax   taxes

5. The flowers were in a large _____ .   basket   baskets

★ Word Study · Lesson 17

Plurals

Type of Plural	Examples
Most plural nouns have an *s* at the end.	books
Nouns that end in *sh*, *ch*, *x*, *s*, or *ss* have *es* at the end for their plural form.	dishes, lunches, boxes, circuses, guesses
Nouns that end in a consonant and *y* drop the *y* and have *ies* at the end for their plural form.	pennies

E Complete the chart below with the missing forms of each word.

	Singular Noun	Plural Noun
1.	trophy	
2.		recesses
3.	index	
4.	coach	
5.	creature	
6.		wishes

F Read the paragraphs and circle the plural nouns. Then answer the questions.

A few science classes from our school visited the zoo yesterday. Our first stop was to see the hippopotamuses. We also saw some lion cubs. They were cute, but it would be wrong to think of them as cuddly kitties! The walruses entertained us with their diving, and the ostriches just stared. In one display, we saw butterflies. Another building housed birds from all over. They were either flying around or hopping on their perches.

Back at school, our teacher showed us atlases, and we looked up the countries from which many of the animals came.

1. Why do you think the students visited the zoo? _____

2. What were the largest animals they saw? _____

3. Why did the students look at atlases? _____

Extra Practice . . . Word Study © 2010 by Linda Ward Beech, Scholastic Teaching Resources

★ Word Study · Lesson 18

More Plurals

The plural form of a noun is usually spelled differently than the singular form. When you read, look to see if a noun is singular or plural.

Type of Plural	Examples
Nouns that end in *f* or *fe* usually change those letters to *ves* for their plural form.	leaves, wives
Some nouns have irregular plurals.	men
Some nouns have the same spelling in their singular and plural forms.	deer, moose, fowl

A Study the chart above. Then use it to find and circle the plural noun in each sentence.

1. Josie cut the apple into halves.

2. The two chairmen met to discuss the problem.

3. The display had eight reindeer in it.

4. The salesmen in the store were all busy.

5. How many lives did the doctor save?

6. The women attended a meeting.

B Write the plural form of each word below. Use a dictionary to help you.

1. child   _____

2. salmon   _____

3. trout   _____

4. foot   _____

5. ox   _____

6. tooth   _____

7. sheep   _____

8. mouse   _____

Extra Practice . . . Word Study © 2010 by Linda Ward Beech, Scholastic Teaching Resources

★ Word Study · Lesson 18

More Plurals

Type of Plural	Examples
Nouns that end in *f* or *fe* usually change those letters to *ves* for their plural form.	leaves, wives
Some nouns have irregular plurals.	men
Some nouns have the same spelling in their singular and plural forms.	deer, moose, fowl

C Fill in the circle next to the word that best tells about each picture.

1.
   ○ loaf
   ○ leaf
   ○ loaves

2.
   ○ man
   ○ men
   ○ mens

3.
   ○ feets
   ○ foot
   ○ feet

4.
   ○ calf
   ○ calfs
   ○ calves

5.
   ○ wolf
   ○ wolves
   ○ worlds

6.
   ○ scarf
   ○ scarfs
   ○ scarves

D Circle the correct word to complete each sentence.

1. In the fall we have to rake so many _____ .   leaf   leaves

2. We went down to the _____ to see the boats.   wharf   wharves

3. How many _____ are in that fairy tale?   elf   elves

4. The wagon was pulled by a team of _____ .   ox   oxen

5. Did you know there are _____ in the barn?   mouse   mice

Extra Practice . . . Word Study © 2010 by Linda Ward Beech, Scholastic Teaching Resources

★ Word Study · Lesson 18

More Plurals

Type of Plural	Examples
Nouns that end in *f* or *fe* usually change those letters to *ves* for their plural form.	leaves, wives
Some nouns have irregular plurals.	men
Some nouns have the same spelling in their singular and plural forms.	deer, moose, fowl

Complete the chart below with the missing form of each word.

	Singular Noun	Plural Noun
1.	fowl	
2.		selves
3.	thief	
4.		salmon
5.	knife	
6.	child	

Read the paragraphs and circle the plural nouns. Then answer the questions.

My grandfather gave the children in our family a painting. It is a farm scene with oxen, sheep, and fowl, such as geese, in a barnyard. Two calves stand near the fence, their hooves deep in mud.

On the outside of the fence is a tree with dark green leaves. Beneath the tree are two wolves. Will these thieves attack? Will their sharp teeth take the lives in the barnyard? This painting has always made me think.

1. What kind of scene does the painting show? _____

2. What is the danger lurking in the picture? _____

_____

3. Why does the painting make the writer think? _____

_____

★ Word Study · Lesson 19

Plurals and Possessives

When you read, be sure not to confuse plural nouns with possessive nouns. Possessive nouns show ownership and have an apostrophe.

Kind of Possessive	Examples	Meaning
Singular possessive nouns end in an apostrophe (') and s.	the dog's bone Manny's hat	bone belonging to the dog hat belonging to Manny
Most plural possessive nouns end in s and an apostrophe (').	the girls' house the pennies' luster	house belonging to the girls luster of the pennies
Plural nouns that do not end in s end in an apostrophe (') and s.	the women's coats	coats belonging to the women

A **Study the chart above. Then read each sentence and underline the possessive noun. Write S or P to tell if the possessive noun is singular or plural.**

1. We saw the lions' den at the zoo.   _____

2. The author's voice is very clear in this book.   _____

3. The men's feet were very dirty from the muddy field.   _____

4. Was the story's ending a surprise to you?   _____

5. The players' equipment is ready to be loaded onto the buses.   _____

B **Read each sentence. Then tell who the owner is and what belongs to the owner.**

	Owner	What Is Owned
1. Tessa's dog ran away yesterday.		
2. Did you borrow the boys' sled?		
3. The berries' color is a brilliant blue.		
4. Mom wanted to look at the children's clothes.		
5. These are my friend's mice.		

Extra Practice . . . Word Study © 2010 by Linda Ward Beech, Scholastic Teaching Resources

★ Word Study · Lesson 19

Plurals and Possessives

Kind of Possessive	Examples	Meaning
Singular possessive nouns end in an apostrophe (') and s.	the dog's bone Manny's hat	bone belonging to the dog hat belonging to Manny
Most plural possessive nouns end in s and an apostrophe (').	the girls' house the pennies' luster	house belonging to the girls luster of the pennies
Plural nouns that do not end in s end in an apostrophe (') and s.	the women's coats	coats belonging to the women

C **Read each sentence. Then write any plural nouns or possessive nouns you find.**

	Plural Nouns	Possessive Nouns
1. The girls tried not to walk on the neighbor's lawn.		
2. The doctors' offices are on that street.		
3. A lot of relatives are coming to my aunt's party.		
4. The men's team lost two games.		
5. A spider's web can trap many insects.		

D **Write a sentence using each of the words below.**

1. reindeers' _____

2. Craig's _____

3. sidewalks' _____

4. daisy's _____

5. puppies' _____

Name _____   Date _____

★ Word Study · Lesson 19

Plurals and Possessives

Kind of Possessive	Examples	Meaning
Singular possessive nouns end in an apostrophe (') and s.	the dog's bone Manny's hat	bone belonging to the dog hat belonging to Manny
Most plural possessive nouns end in s and an apostrophe (').	the girls' house the pennies' luster	house belonging to the girls luster of the pennies
Plural nouns that do not end in s end in an apostrophe (') and s.	the women's coats	coats belonging to the women

E **Circle the correct word to complete each sentence.**

1. At the farm the guests rode on ____ .   ponies   pony's   ponies'

2. We read several ____ diaries in history class.   explorers   explorers'   explorer's

3. The ____ point was not sharp enough.   pencils   pencil's   pencils'

4. He entered the ____ locker room.   mens   mens'   men's

5. Julie loved the way that ____ hair was done.   actress'   actresses   actress's

F **Read the paragraph and circle the possessive nouns. Then answer the questions.**

In the field behind our neighbor's garage is a bluebird's house. Some workers from the Nature Society's headquarters put it up last spring. We use my father's binoculars to watch the scene. Since the birds' nest is in the little house, it's hard to see the mother's eggs. We can hear the parents scolding, though, when someone gets too near.

1. Where is the birdhouse? _____

_____

2. Why is it hard to see the birds? _____

_____

3. Why don't the birds want anyone near the house? _____

_____

Extra Practice . . . Word Study © 2010 by Linda Ward Beech, Scholastic Teaching Resources

★ Word Study · Lesson 20

Word Endings

When an ending is added to a word, the word's meaning changes. Pay attention to word endings when you read.

Part of Speech	Ending	Form	Example
verb	-ed	past tense (action takes place in past)	walk + ed = walked
adjective or adverb	-er	comparative (compares 2 things)	tall + er = taller
adjective or adverb	-est	superlative (compares more than 2 things)	tall + est = tallest

A Study the chart above. Then read each sentence and underline the verb, adjective, or adverb with an ending. Write the form of the word on the line.

1. Delaware is smaller than Vermont.   _____

2. Winter is the coldest season.   _____

3. One clown tossed a pie at a second clown.   _____

4. Della opened the bedroom window.   _____

5. Those geese make the loudest sound I have ever heard.   _____

6. The boy dove deeper than his friend did.   _____

B Read each question. Then circle the best answer.

1. Which one has already happened?   a. **pull**   b. **puller**   c. **pulled**

2. Which one is fastest?   a. **quicker**   b. **quickest**   c. **quick**

3. Which one compares two temperatures? a. **warm**   b. **warmer**   c. **warmest**

4. Which one is the highest?   a. **tall**   b. **taller**   c. **tallest**

5. Which sound is over?   a. **roared**   b. **roar**   c. **roars**

★ Word Study · Lesson 20

Word Endings

Part of Speech	Ending	Form	Example
verb	-ed	past tense (action takes place in past)	walk + ed = walked
adjective or adverb	-er	comparative (compares 2 things)	tall + er = taller
adjective or adverb	-est	superlative (compares more than 2 things)	tall + est = tallest

C **Circle the correct word to complete each sentence.**

1. That was the ____ test we ever had.   harder   hardest

2. Is Jessica ____ than Emily?   older   oldest

3. The train left ____ than expected.   later   latest

4. Elm Street is ____ than Oak Street.   narrower   narrowest

5. Wade is the ____ runner in the class.   fast   fastest

6. The tree in the middle grew the ____ of all.   straighter   straightest

D **Fill in the circle next to the word that best tells about each picture.**

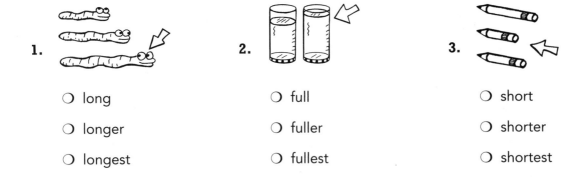

1.
○ long
○ longer
○ longest

2.
○ full
○ fuller
○ fullest

3.
○ short
○ shorter
○ shortest

Extra Practice . . . Word Study © 2010 by Linda Ward Beech, Scholastic Teaching Resources

★ Word Study · Lesson 20

Word Endings

Part of Speech	Ending	Form	Example
verb	-ed	past tense (action takes place in past)	walk + ed = walked
adjective or adverb	-er	comparative (compares 2 things)	tall + er = taller
adjective or adverb	-est	superlative (compares more than 2 things)	tall + est = tallest

E **Write a sentence using each of the words below.**

1. explained _____

2. lighter _____

3. heaped _____

4. greatest _____

5. danced _____

F **Read the clues, then complete the puzzle.**

1. past tense of *wait*   W _ _ _ _ _

2. comparative form of *strong*   _ _ _ O _ _ _ _

3. superlative form of *bright*   _ R _ _ _ _ _ _ _

4. superlative form of *dark*   D _ _ _ _ _ _

5. past tense of *help*   _ E _ _ _ _

6. past tense of *answer*   _ N _ _ _ _ _ _

7. past tense of *add*   _ _ D _ _

8. comparative form of *wild*   _ I _ _ _ _

9. superlative form of *soon*   _ _ _ N _ _ _

10. past tense of *gobble*   G _ _ _ _ _ _

★ Word Study · Lesson 21

Contractions

A contraction is formed when two words are put together and some letters are left out. An apostrophe (') replaces the missing letters.

Words	Contractions
I am	I'm
is not	isn't
do not	don't

A **Underline the contraction in each sentence. Then write the two words that make up the contraction.**

1. We'll have dinner at six tonight.   _____   _____

2. When you're in town, please buy me a paper.   _____   _____

3. Sara can't come to the party.   _____   _____

4. That wasn't a good joke.   _____   _____

5. How's your mother feeling?   _____   _____

6. Ask Mac to tell us when he'll be here.   _____   _____

B **Draw a line to match each pair of words to its contraction.**

1. were not   a. **she'd**

2. we have   b. **won't**

3. she would   c. **there's**

4. will not   d. **weren't**

5. has not   e. **hasn't**

6. there is   f. **we've**

7. must not   g. **should've**

8. should have   h. **mustn't**

★ Word Study · Lesson 21

Contractions

Words	Contractions
I am	I'm
is not	isn't
do not	don't

C **Write a contraction for each set of words below.**

1. we would _____
2. I have _____
3. we are _____
4. does not _____
5. she is _____

6. where is _____
7. they have _____
8. let us _____
9. I will _____
10. he had _____

D **Circle a pair of words in each sentence that could form a contraction. Then write the contraction.**

1. If you will call me, we can plan our shopping trip. _____

2. Nora can not finish her paper on time. _____

3. Where is the dish I use for the cat? _____

4. Mr. Foster found the place where they have been digging. _____

5. The guests have not been served dinner yet. _____

6. Please do not walk on the clean floor with dirty shoes. _____

★ Word Study · Lesson 21

Contractions

Words	Contractions
I am	I'm
is not	isn't
do not	don't

E **Read each question. Then circle the best answer.**

1. Which one is negative?   a. **you're**   b. **aren't**   c. **that's**

2. Which one is short for *will*?   a. **they'd**   b. **they've**   c. **they'll**

3. Which one is in the present?   a. **she's**   b. **she'd**   c. **she'll**

4. Which one is in the past?   a. **hadn't**   b. **hasn't**   c. **isn't**

5. Which one is in the future?   a. **I'd**   b. **I'll**   c. **I'm**

F **Read the paragraph and circle the words with contractions. Then answer the questions.**

> We're rushing around the house in a giddy mood. My parents haven't said anything, but I know they'll soon speak out. I'm not sure what I'll tell them. There's really nothing very funny happening. It's just that exams are over, and that's such a relief. My brother can't stop singing, and he doesn't have a very good voice. Wendy's hopeless with laughter. She's making me giggle too. I guess we've all been under a lot of stress.

1. Why are the kids in a giddy mood? _____

   _____

2. Why might their parents wonder what's going on? _____

   _____

3. What causes you to get silly? _____

   _____

★ Word Study · Lesson 22

Easily Confused Words

Some words sound alike and are easily confused.

Easily Confused Words	Contraction	Possessive
you're and your	Call us when you're home.	Here is your hat.
it's and its	I think it's late.	What is its name?
who's and whose	Who's coming with me?	Whose painting is that?
they're and their	They're at the seashore.	The students read their books.

A Study the chart above. Then read each sentence and write Contraction or Possessive to identify the underlined word.

1. Is that your sister <u>who's</u> in the kitchen? _____

2. The singers will stand when it is <u>their</u> turn to perform. _____

3. The dog scratched <u>its</u> head. _____

4. Maud thinks <u>it's</u> too late to take a walk. _____

5. Are these <u>your</u> mittens? _____

6. I wonder <u>whose</u> car is in our driveway. _____

7. The Bentons said <u>they're</u> giving a party. _____

8. I hope <u>you're</u> feeling better. _____

B Circle the correct word to complete each sentence.

1. Carmine got a new skateboard, and _____ great.   its   it's

2. Do you think _____ going to win this game?   they're   their

3. Dad, _____ away on business, sent me a postcard.   who's   whose

4. The cow flicked _____ tail.   its   it's

5. Let us know if _____ going to need a ride.   you're   your

★ Word Study · Lesson 22

Easily Confused Words

Easily Confused Words	Contraction	Possessive
you're and your	Call us when you're home.	Here is your hat.
it's and its	I think it's late.	What is its name?
who's and whose	Who's coming with me?	Whose painting is that?
they're and their	They're at the seashore.	The students read their books.

C **Find the mistake in each sentence below. Then rewrite the sentence so it is correct.**

1. Do you think its too hot to go to your dance class? _____

_____

2. Your going to be sorry for breaking their glass. _____

_____

3. I think their going to visit the people whose dog got loose. _____

_____

4. Whose the actress in the show with your uncle? _____

_____

5. Their team won it's first game this season. _____

_____

D **Write a sentence using each of the words below.**

1. whose _____

2. their _____

3. your _____

4. it's _____

5. you're _____

★ Word Study · Lesson 22

Easily Confused Words

Easily Confused Words	Contraction	Possessive
you're and your	Call us when you're home.	Here is your hat.
it's and its	I think it's late.	What is its name?
who's and whose	Who's coming with me?	Whose painting is that?
they're and their	They're at the seashore.	The students read their books.

E **Read each question. Then circle the best answer.**

1. Which one is a contraction?   a. **they're**   b. **there**   c. **their**

2. Which one is a possessive?   a. **whose**   b. **who**   c. **who's**

3. Which one means "belonging to you"?   a. **you**   b. **you're**   c. **your**

4. Which one is two words together?   a. **its**   b. **it**   c. **it's**

5. Which one means "you are"?   a. **you**   b. **your**   c. **you're**

F **Read the paragraphs and circle the words from this lesson. Then answer the questions.**

    It's been a busy morning for Rowdy. First he had to wake Paul, in whose room he sleeps. Then they played their usual game of tug-the-blanket.

    "Who's ready for breakfast?" called Paul's mom. "It's late," she said. "Hurry, or you're going to miss the bus. And don't forget your math book!"

    Paul and Rowdy raced to the bus stop just as the bus came into view, its warning lights blinking. Once Paul was on the bus, Rowdy went home. He looked for his toys. "They're in your box," Paul's mother told him. Rowdy found his monkey and grabbed it by its tail. He played for awhile and then took a nap.

1. Who is Rowdy? _____

2. How does Rowdy's day differ from Paul's? _____

_____

3. Where do you think Rowdy will be when Paul comes home? _____

_____

★ Word Study · Lesson 23

Syllables

Words can be divided into syllables. A syllable has one vowel sound. You can use syllables to help you break down an unfamiliar word for reading and pronunciation. Syllables have different spelling patterns. In many words, each syllable ends in a consonant.

Word	Number of Vowel Sounds	Number of Syllables	Example
can	1 vowel sound	1 syllable	can
candid	2 vowel sounds	2 syllables	can did

A **Count the vowel sounds and write the number of syllables in each word below.**

1. zigzag _____

2. yelled _____

3. magnet _____

4. dug _____

5. pocket _____

6. wonderful _____

7. bent _____

8. puppet _____

9. singing _____

10. cucumber _____

11. different _____

12. atlas _____

B **Read each word below. Write the two syllables in the word. Use a dictionary to help you.**

1. contest _____ _____

2. tidbit _____ _____

3. fossil _____ _____

4. attic _____ _____

5. velvet _____ _____

6. cutlet _____ _____

7. robin _____ _____

8. victim _____ _____

9. picnic _____ _____

10. blister _____ _____

★ Word Study · Lesson 23

Syllables

Word	Number of Vowel Sounds	Number of Syllables	Example
can	1 vowel sound	1 syllable	can
candid	2 vowel sounds	2 syllables	can did

C Add the syllable on the left to each syllable in the row to form new words.

1. sun   _____tan   _____down   _____set

2. com   _____mon   _____et   _____ic

3. den   _____im   _____tist   _____tal

4. sad   _____dle   _____der   _____den

5. can   _____yon   _____vas   _____cer

D For each group of syllables below, add a syllable from the box to form new words.

mit   tor   et   son

1. rock + _____   3. sub + _____

   tick + _____   ad + _____

   blank + _____   trans + _____

2. trac + _____   4. crim + _____

   hec + _____   les + _____

   fac + _____   ar + _____

★ Word Study · Lesson 23

Syllables

Word	Number of Vowel Sounds	Number of Syllables	Example
can	1 vowel sound	1 syllable	can
candid	2 vowel sounds	2 syllables	can did

E **Read the clue and circle the correct word.**

1. I am a compound word with two syllables.   a. **caterpillar**   b. **catnip**   c. **cat**

2. I am a two-syllable word with a prefix.   a. **expect**   b. **expected**   c. **even**

3. I am a three-syllable word with a suffix.   a. **amaze**   b. **maze**   c. **amazement**

4. I am a one-syllable word with a long vowel sound.   a. **main**   b. **man**   c. **maintain**

5. I am a two-syllable word in plural form.   a. **penny**   b. **pennies**   c. **pen**

F **Read the paragraph and circle at least five two-syllable words. Then answer the questions.**

Mr. Matlet approached his favorite bench. His steps were slow and halting, but he was in no rush. Settling onto the wooden bench, he looked at the summer scene. The basketball courts were buzzing with pickup games as kids from the nearby apartments jostled for the ball. A small child pointed as her mother pushed her by in a stroller. A couple went by holding hands. The singsong chant of a jumprope game could be heard from one corner. Mr. Matlet nodded and grinned as he opened his paper.

1. Where is Mr. Matlet? _____

2. How does he feel about the place? _____

_____

3. Has he been here before? Explain. _____

_____

4. A good title for this paragraph would be _____ .

★ Word Study · Lesson 24

More Syllables

Words can be divided into syllables. A syllable has one vowel sound. You can use syllables to help you break down an unfamiliar word for reading and pronunciation. Syllables have different spelling patterns. Many words end in a consonant followed by a vowel sound spelled *-le, -al,* or *-el*.

Word	Number of Vowel Sounds	Number of Syllables	Example
global	2 vowel sounds	2 syllables	glob al
middle	2 vowel sounds	2 syllables	mid dle
rebel	2 vowel sounds	2 syllables	re bel

A Count the vowel sounds and write the number of syllables in each word below.

1. fable _____

2. jumble _____

3. maternal _____

4. illegal _____

5. pedal _____

6. bugle _____

7. curable _____

8. fizzle _____

9. nickel _____

10. mislabel _____

11. rental _____

12. unable _____

B Read each word below. Write the two syllables in the word. Use a dictionary to help you.

1. jingle _____ _____

2. petal _____ _____

3. vocal _____ _____

4. swivel _____ _____

5. sample _____ _____

6. twinkle _____ _____

7. chapel _____ _____

8. jackal _____ _____

9. mussel _____ _____

10. battle _____ _____

★ Word Study · Lesson 24

More Syllables

Word	Number of Vowel Sounds	Number of Syllables	Example
global	2 vowel sounds	2 syllables	glob al
middle	2 vowel sounds	2 syllables	mid dle
rebel	2 vowel sounds	2 syllables	re bel

C Add the syllable on the left to each syllable in the row to form new words.

1. **ble**   scrib_____   mar_____   wob_____

2. **el**   mod_____   shriv_____   chis_____

3. **tal**   men_____   bru_____   por_____

4. **gle**   gog_____   jun_____   bea_____

5. **tle**   bus_____   set_____   tat_____

D Read the clue and circle the correct word.

1. I am a two-syllable word that ends in *zle*.   a. **sizzling**   b. **sizzle**   c. **sizzled**

2. I am a two-syllable word that ends in *al*.   a. **gerbil**   b. **yokel**   c. **local**

3. I am a three-syllable word that ends in *ble*.   a. **remember**   b. **resemble**   c. **regal**

4. I am a two-syllable word that ends in *nel*.   a. **kernel**   b. **journal**   c. **snivel**

5. I am a four-syllable word that ends in *el*.   a. **mislabel**   b. **vehicle**   c. **pumpernickel**

★ Word Study · Lesson 24

More Syllables

Word	Number of Vowel Sounds	Number of Syllables	Example
global	2 vowel sounds	2 syllables	glob al
middle	2 vowel sounds	2 syllables	mid dle
rebel	2 vowel sounds	2 syllables	re bel

E Below are some common syllables. For each syllable, write two words that include that syllable. Use a dictionary to check your work.

1. _____

2. _____

3. _____

4. _____

5. _____

ing
er
un
ny
re

F Read the paragraph and circle at least five two-syllable words and five three-syllable words. Then answer the questions.

      The Riddlesons went to the state fair on Wednesday. Jack was full of excitement and ran straight to see the farm animals. The horses, cattle, pigs, and sheep were in big barns. Sara got a popsicle on a stick, and Mom bought some homemade apple strudel. Uncle Mike won a bunch of purple balloons at a game booth. The whole family rode on the carousel, but only Sara and her dad were brave enough to go on the Rattling Roller Coaster.

1. In what season do you think the state fair was held? Why? _____

_____

2. What did Jack see first? _____

3. Who do you think is older, Sara or Jack? Why? _____

_____

Answer Key

LESSON 1

Page 6: A. 1.–10. ant + hill = anthill, tea + pot = teapot, barn + yard = barnyard, bird + cage = birdcage, clothes + pin = clothespin, door + mat = doormat, pop + corn = popcorn, snow + flake = snowflake, tool + box = toolbox, wheel + chair = wheelchair **B.** 1. bedroom, bedtime, bedspread 2. snowsuit, snowstorm, snowplow 3. footprint, footpath, footstool 4. eyelid, eyesight, eyeball **Page 7: C.** 1. cookbook, notebook, pocketbook 2. greenhouse, birdhouse, lighthouse 3. someday, everyday, birthday 4. tugboat, sailboat, motorboat **D.** 1. bookcase 2. flowerpot 3. mailbox 4. doghouse 5. rowboat 6. newspaper **Page 8: E.** 1. horsefly 2. matchbox 3. catfish 4. sunrise 5. seaweed 6. daydream 7. haircut 8. doorstep 9. bedroll 10. milkshake **F.** hallway, beachball, baseball, football, basketball, skateboard, snowboard 1. She likes sports. 2. She keeps them in a box in the hall. 3. She likes skateboarding and snowboarding.

LESSON 2

Page 9: A. 1. foot, note 2. pipe, line 3. bar, bell 4. grass, hopper 5. play, pen 6. law, maker 7. home, owner 8. ground, work **B.** 1. shirtsleeve 2. bearskin 3. wallpaper 4. bathrobe 5. bridegroom 6. armchair 7. hillside 8. database **Page 10: C.** 1. bookshop 2. beanstalk 3. honeycomb 4. heartbreak 5. artwork 6. billfold **D.** 1. c 2. a 3. c 4. c 5. c 6. b 7. b 8. b 9. c 10. b **Page 11: E.** 1. bookmark 2. tabletop 3. sandbox 4. barefoot 5. goldfish 6. sunburn 7. snowball 8. copycat 9. fireplace 10. applesauce **F.** teaspoon, tablespoon, potholder, everything, cookbook, setback, birthday, homemade 1. It was for his mother's birthday. 2. It went well except for when Kirk spilled some batter. 3. Answers will vary.

LESSON 3

Page 12: A. 1. overcook 2. redo 3. unfair 4. subway 5. mistreat **B.** 1. un, fold 2. mis, use 3. un, safe 4. re, pack 5. sub, marine 6. over, ripe 7. mis, step 8. un, sure 9. sub, plot, 10. over, eat 11. re, tie 12. re, write **Page 13: C.** 1. over; do too much, tip too much, bake too much 2. re; heat again, fill again, tell again 3. un; not real, not happy, not kind 4. mis; name incorrectly, lead in a wrong way, number in a wrong way **D.** 1. recall 2. uneven 3. overflow 4. subsoil 5. misread **Page 14: E.** 1. b 2. a 3. c 4. a 5. c **F.** unseen, overslept, misjudged, subtitle, unsure, restate 1. It happens in a school. 2. He asked Alice a question. 3. She came in late and doesn't know where the class is in the book.

LESSON 4

Page 15: A. 1. informal 2. disobey 3. underpay 4. defrost 5. forewarn **B.** 1. in; not direct 2. de; take away control 3. dis; not like 4. under, below age 5. fore, tell beforehand 6. dis, not honest 7. fore; in the front 8. de; take from a throne 9. under; too few clothes **Page 16: C.** 1. b 2. a 3. c 4. c 5. b **D.** 1. incorrect 2. defog 3. undercharge 4. displease 5. foresee **Page 17: E.** 1. c 2. b 3. a 4. a 5. b **F.** forenoon, underbody, disabled, insane, discontinue, disembark, foremost 1. It got stuck in the weeds. 2. He seemed upset. 3. Mom said to put on life jackets.

LESSON 5

Page 18: A. 1. multilayered 2. preview 3. improper 4. superstar 5. semicircle **B.** 1. semiprecious 2. impure 3. multinational 4. supermarket 5. pregame **Page 19: C.** 1. imperfect 2. superman 3. prejudge 4. semicolon 5. multicolored **D.** 1. immature, impossible, impatient 2. semifinal, semiannual, semimonthly 3. superfine, superhuman, supernatural **Page 20: E.** 1. b 2. a 3. c 4. a 5. a **F.** 1. semicircle 2. multicultural 3. impatient 4. semisweet 5. predate 6. superwoman 7. impolite 8. preheat 9. multimedia 10. preschool

LESSON 6

Page 21: A. 1. writer 2. sadly 3. washable 4. rudeness 5. joyful **B.** 1. ful, grace 2. ly, fond 3. er, teach 4. able, comfort 5. ful, pain 6. ness, fair 7. or, direct 8. ly, weak 9. ful, skill 10. ness, dark 11. er, lead 12, ly, sweet **Page 22: C.** 1. ful: full of grace, full of hope, full of cheer 2. ly: in a rapid way, in a neat way, in a quiet way 3. able: can be fixed, can be drunk, can be beaten 4. er: person who is a banker, person who is a builder, person who is a climber **D.** 1. inventor 2. quickly 3. shyness 4. careful 5. breakable **Page 23: E.** 1. b 2. a 3. b 4. c 5. b **F.** 1. tightly 2. warmly 3. swiftly 4. darkly 5. brokenly 6. bitingly 7. sweetly 8. absently

LESSON 7

Page 24: A. 1. organist 2. cloudless 3. leaky 4. movement 5. hardship **B.** 1. ageless, faceless, careless 2. placement, treatment, agreement 3. misty, woody, gloomy **Page 25: C.** 1. colorless 2. rainy 3. development 4. leadership 5. violinist **D.** 1. nameless 2. journalist 3. steamy 4. appointment 5. friendship **Page 26: E.** 1. b 2. a 3. b 4. c 5. b **F.** naturalist, contentment, timeless, environment, lucky, enjoyment, internship, ranger, leafy, arrangement 1. She finds great contentment in it. 2. He describes a desert and a forest environment. 3. Answers will vary. Possible: It is cooler.

LESSON 8

Page 27: A. 1. collection 2. assistant 3. seasonal 4. knighthood 5. marvelous **B.** 1. -al, clinic 2. -ant, defend 3. -ion, protect 4. -ant, attend 5. -hood, adult 6. -al, nation 7. -ous, joy 8. -ous, humor 9. -ion, reject 10. -hood, sister 11. -al, comic 12. -ion, act **Page 28: C.** 1. contestant 2. coastal 3. childhood 4. dangerous 5. attraction **D.** 1. motherhood 2. original 3. correction 4. adventurous 5. president

Page 29: E. 1. b 2. a 3. a 4. c 5. b **F.** boyhood, servant, thunderous, champion, reaction, educational, knighthood 1. He was a servant to a knight. 2. The knight was loud and good at fighting. 3. The boy wanted to become a knight.

LESSON 9

Page 30: A. 1. re-, -ion, act 2. non-, -er, smoke 3. un-, -able, sink 4. over-, -ment, pay 5. fore-, -able, see 6. dis-, -ment, agree 7. un-, -able, beat 8. in-, -ness, direct 9. non-, -er, support 10. mis-, -ment, treat **B.** 1. returnable 2. renewal 3. unkindness 4. repayment 5. imperfection **Page 31: C.** 1. nonpayment, unreadable, unevenness, unfairness, immovable 2. unevenness, unfairness 3. forerunner, preschooler, prepayment **D.** 1. b 2. a 3. c 4. a 5. c **Page 32: E.** 1. b 2. c 3. a 4. b 5. c **F.** unbreakable, imperfection, replacement, disapproval, unusable, unhappiness, impatiently 1. There is a rip in one of the cups. 2. He is disapproving. 3. She is unhappy and impatient.

LESSON 10

Page 33: A. 1. porter 2. pedal 3. artist 4. action 5. numeral **B.** 1. art; something done with skill 2. ped; a person on foot 3. numer; many in number 4. act; showing action 5. port; something that can be carried **C.** 1. pedestal 2. transport 3. artisan **Page 34: D.** 1. import, deport 2. pedicure, pedometer 3. artificial, artful, 4. acting, activist, activism, transact 5. enumerate, numerical, numerology **E.** 1. c 2. a 3. b 4. c 5. b **Page 35: F.** 1. portfolio 2. pedaling 3. artwork 4. numerical 5. reaction 6. exports 7. artmobile 8. moped 9. actor 10. numbers

LESSON 11

Page 36: A. 1. navy 2. manual 3. population 4. reject 5. formula **B.** 1. inject, rejection, projection 2. manage, manufacture 3. transform, deform, formation **Page 37: C.** 1. eject 2. manicure 3. populous 4. formation 5. naval **D.** 1. pop; b 2. form; a 3. man; c 4. nav; b 5. ject; c **Page 38: E.** 1. a 2. b 3. a 4. c 5. b **F.** manicure, transform, formal, naval, Navy, uniform, manicurist, popular, reject 1. She wanted a haircut and a manicure 2. She had a date with an officer for a formal dinner on the naval base. 3. She was treated well.

LESSON 12

Page 39: A. 1. liberty 2. vision 3. marina 4. audio 5. predict **B.** 1. mariner, maritime 2. liberate, liberal 3. audible, auditory 4. dictate, prediction 5. vista, video **Page 40: C.** 1. dict; b 2. mar; a 3. aud; b 4. vis; c 5. liber; b **D.** 1. dictionary 2. inaudible 3. liberator 4. marinate 5. visible **Page 41: E.** 1. c 2. a 3. a 4. b 5. b **F.** audible, liberated, audition, television, predict, marina, envisioned 1. Her cat got stuck in a tree. 2. She was going to a TV audition. 3. Answers will vary.

LESSON 13

Page 42: A. 1. thermometer 2. geography 3. phonics 4. thermometer 5. geography **B.** 1. geologist 2. speedometer 3. earphones 4. metronome 5. telephone **Page 43: C.** 1. geo; a globelike stone with crystals in it 2. meter; an instrument that measures the distance traveled by vehicles 3. phon; a device that makes the voice louder 4. meter; the measurement of an outer boundary of an area 5. geo; science of earth's crust **D.** 1. phone; a 2. meter; b 3. geo; c 4. phon; b 5. meter; b **Page 44: E.** 1. centimeter; one hundredth of a meter 2. kilometer; one thousand meters 3. diameter; a straight line through the center of a circle 4. millimeter; one thousandth of a meter **F.** phonometer, geometry, geography, phone, perimeter, megaphone 1. It is an instrument that measures sound. 2. He wants to measure the sound his siblings make when they do their homework. 3. Answers will vary.

LESSON 14

Page 45: A. 1. automobile 2. biology 3. photograph 4. biology 5. automobile **B.** 1. autograph 2. biography 3. autocade 4. photocopier 5. biohazard **Page 46: C.** 1. bio; a 2. photo; b 3. auto; c 4. auto; c 5. bio; b **D.** 1. biopsy, biosphere, biological, biofeedback 2. telephoto, photostat, photocopy, photoplay, photographer 3. automation, autobus, automat **Page 47: E.** 1. c 2. c 3. b 4. a 5. c **F.** photographer, automobiles, autographs, biology, biochemistry, biography 1. They were studying about careers. 2. Possible; drawing skills, engineering skills, knowledge of cars 3. Answers will vary.

LESSON 15

Page 48: A. 1. cycle 2. autograph 3. telescope 4. cycle 5. telescope **B.** 1. cycle; to use again 2. tele; a photo taken from a far distance 3. tele; speaking over a distance 4. graph: relating to written or pictorial representation 5. graph; a carbon material used in pencils **Page 49: C.** 1. televise 2. cyclical 3. telegram 4. graphology 5. cyclist **D.** 1. geo; graph 2. tele; graph 3. auto; graph 4. tele; meter 5. tele; photo **E.** 1. b 2. a 3. c 4. b **Page 50: F.** 1. phonograph 2. biography 3. bicycle 4. graphic 5. telephone 6. telegraph 7. telescope 8. autograph 9. televise 10. bicyclist

LESSON 16

Page 51: A. 1. three 2. four 3. hundred 4. one 5. one 6. two 7. ten **B.** 1. cent; hundred 2. bi; two 3. mono; one 4. tri; three 5. bi; two 6. uni; one 7. tri; three **Page 52: C.** 1. centenarian 2. trident 3. unanimous 4. monocle 5. quadruplet 6. bilingual 7. decagon **D.** 1. four 2. one 3. one 4. three 5. ten 6. hundred **Page 53: E.** 1. c 2. b 3. b 4. b 5. a **F.** centennial, uniforms, binoculars, quartet, trio, unicycle, monologue 1. It is celebrating its centennial. 2. He will borrow binoculars. 3. in one hundred years

LESSON 17

Page 54: A. 1. dishes 2. peaches 3. stories 4. buses 5. boys 6. glasses 7. mailboxes **B.** 1. berries 2. messes 3. mixes 4. computers 5. matches 6. octopuses 7. eyelashes 8. hobbies **Page 55: C.** 1. puppies 2. brush 3. foxes 4. walruses 5. churches 6. dresses **D.** 1. melodies 2. beach 3. witnesses 4. taxes 5. basket **Page 56: E.** 1. trophies 2. recess 3. indexes 4. coaches 5. creatures 6. wish **F.** classes, hippopotamuses, cubs, kitties, walruses, ostriches, butterflies, birds, perches, atlases, countries, animals 1. Most likely, the trip was part of their science study. 2. hippopotamuses 3. They were locating the homelands of the animals.

LESSON 18

Page 57: A. 1. halves 2. chairmen 3. reindeer 4. salesmen 5. lives 6. women **B.** 1. children 2. salmon 3. trout 4. feet 5. oxen 6. teeth 7. sheep 8. mice **Page 58: C.** 1. loaves 2. man 3. foot 4. calves 5. wolves 6. scarves **D.** 1. leaves 2. wharf 3. elves 4. oxen 5. mice **Page 59: E.** 1. fowl 2. self 3. thieves 4. salmon 5. knives 6. children **F.** children, oxen, sheep, fowl, geese, calves, hooves, leaves, wolves, thieves, teeth, lives 1. It shows a farm scene. 2.There are two wolves nearby. 3. The writer probably wonders if the wolves will attack or not.

LESSON 19

Page 60: A. 1. P; lions' 2. S; author's 3. P; men's 4. S; story's 5. P; players' **B.** 1. Tessa; dog 2. boys; sled 3. berries; color 4. children; clothes 5. friend; mice **Page 61: C.** 1. girls; neighbor's 2. offices; doctors' 3. relatives; aunt's 4. games; men's 5. insects; spider's **D.** 1.–5. Sentences will vary. Make sure subjects and verbs agree. **Page 62: E.** 1. ponies 2. explorers' 3. pencil's 4. men's 5. actress's **F.** neighbor's, bluebird's, Society's, father's, birds', mother's 1. It's in a field behind a neighbor's house. 2. They make their nest in the birdhouse. 3. They are protective of their eggs.

LESSON 20

Page 63: A. 1. smaller/comparative 2. coldest/ superlative 3. tossed/past tense 4. opened/past tense 5. loudest/superlative 6. deeper/comparative **B.** 1. c 2. b 3. b 4. c 5. a **Page 64: C.** 1. hardest 2. older 3. later 4. narrower 5. fastest 6. straightest **D.** 1. longest 2. fuller 3. shortest **Page 65: E.** Answers will vary. Check to see that students use the words correctly. **F.** 1. waited 2. stronger 3. brightest 4. darkest 5. helped 6. answered 7. added 8. wilder 9. soonest 10. gobbled

LESSON 21

Page 66: A. 1. we'll/ we will 2. you're/you are 3. can't/ can not 4. wasn't/was not 5. How's/How is 6. he'll/he will **B.** 1. d 2. f 3. a 4. b 5. e 6. c 7. h 8. g **Page 67: C.** 1. we'd 2. I've 3. we're 4. doesn't 5. she's 6. where's 7. they've 8. let's 9. I'll 10. he'd **D.** 1. you will/you'll 2. can not/can't 3. Where is/Where's 4. they

have/they've 5. have not/haven't 6. do not/don't **Page 68: E.** 1. b 2. c 3. a 4. a 5. b **F.** We're, haven't, they'll, I'm, I'll, There's, It's, that's, can't, doesn't, Wendy's, She's, we've 1. They've just finished exams. 2. The kids are acting silly for no apparent reason. 3. Answers will vary.

LESSON 22

Page 69: A. 1. Contraction 2. Possessive 3. Possessive 4. Contraction 5. Possessive 6. Possessive 7. Contraction 8. Contraction **B.** 1. it's 2. they're 3. who's 4. its 5. you're **Page 70: C.** 1. it's 2. You're 3. they're 4. Who's 5. its **D.** Answers will vary. Check to be sure students use the words correctly. **Page 71: E.** 1. a 2. a 3. c 4. c 5. c **F.** It's, whose, their, Who's, It's, you're, your, its, They're, its 1. He is a pet dog who belongs to Paul. 2. Rowdy stays home and plays and naps during the day, while Paul goes to school. 3. He will be at the bus stop waiting for Paul.

LESSON 23

Page 72: A. 1. 2 2. 2 3. 2 4. 1 5. 2 6. 3 7. 1 8. 2 9. 2 10. 3 11. 3 12. 2 **B.** 1. con/test 2. tid/bit 3. fos/sil 4. at/tic 5. vel/vet 6. cut/let 7. rob/in 8. vic/tim 9. pic/ nic 10. blis/ter **Page 73: C.** 1. suntan, sundown, sunset 2. common, comet, comic 3. denim, dentist, dental 4. saddle, sadder, sadden 5. canyon, canvas, cancer **D.** 1. rocket, ticket, blanket 2. tractor, hector, factor 3. submit, admit, transmit 4. crimson, lesson, arson **Page 74: E.** 1. b 2. a 3. c 4. a 5. b **F.** Possible two-syllable words: Matlet, halting, Settling, onto, wooden, looked, summer, buzzing, pickup, nearby, jostled, pointed, mother, pushed, stroller, couple, holding, singsong, jumprope, corner, nodded, grinned, opened, paper 1. He is in a park. 2. He is happy there. 3. Yes, he goes to his favorite bench. 4. Answers will vary. Sample: Mr. Matlet's Favorite Place

LESSON 24

Page 75: A. 1. 2 2. 2 3. 3 4. 3 5. 2 6. 2 7. 3 8. 2 9. 2 10. 3 11. 2 12. 3 **B.** 1. jin/gle 2. pet/al 3. voc/al 4. swiv/el 5. sam/ple 6. twin/kle 7. chap/el 8. jack/al 9. mus/sel 10. bat/tle **Page 76: C.** 1. scribble, marble, wobble 2. model, shrivel, chisel 3. mental, brutal, portal 4. goggle, jungle, beagle 5. bustle, settle, tattle **D.** 1. b 2. c 3. b 4. a 5. c **Page 77: E.** Answers will vary. Sample: 1. helping, singing 2. worker, teacher 3. unfair, undo 4. penny, funny 5. remake, reread **F.** Possible two-syllable words: horses, cattle, Sara, homemade, apple, strudel, Uncle, purple, balloons, enough, Rattling, Roller, Coaster. Possible three-syllable words: Riddlesons, Wednesday, excitement, animals, popsicle, family, carousel 1. Most likely it was summer because the family went on a Wednesday, which is usually a school day. 2. He saw the farm animals. 3. Most likely Sara is older because she went on the roller coaster.